MASTER MIND

ACTION GUIDE

YOUR GUIDE TO ESTABLISHING AND MAINTAINING A SUCCESSFUL MASTER MIND GROUP

AN OFFICIAL PUBLICATION OF
THE NAPOLEON HILL FOUNDATION

Published and Distributed by
SOUND WISDOM
PO Box 310
Shippensburg, PA 17257-0310
717-530-2122
info@soundwisdom.com
www.soundwisdom.com

ISBN 13 TP: 978-1-64095-400-7
ISBN 13 eBook: 978-1-64095-401-4

For Worldwide Distribution, Printed in the U.S.A.
1 2 3 4 5 6 / 22 21 20

Search where you will, wherever you find an outstanding success in business, finance, industry or in any of the professions, you may be sure that back of the success is some individual who has applied the principle of the "Master Mind." These outstanding successes often appear to be the handiwork of but one person, but search closely and the other individuals whose minds have been coordinated with his own may be found.

—Napoleon Hill, *The Law of Success*

TABLE OF CONTENTS

INTRODUCTION
What Is the Master Mind Principle?

No one can build a fortune or attain success entirely by themselves. As Napoleon Hill writes in *The Science of Personal Achievement*, "Nobody ever rises above mediocrity who does not learn to use the brains of other people."[1] It is for this reason that Hill calls the Master Mind principle the "hub" of his entire philosophy of individual achievement, which he presents in *Think and Grow Rich*, *The Law of Success*, and countless other titles.[2] Decades of research and interviews with over five hundred of America's leading entrepreneurs, inventors, and influencers led Hill to seize on the Master Mind principle—which posits that "two or more minds, working together in harmony toward a definite objective, have more power than a single mind"[3]—as the key differentiator between those who achieve their definite major purpose in life and those who do not.

THE MASTER MIND PRINCIPLE
Two or more minds, working together in harmony toward a definite objective, have more power than a single mind.

Hill first discovered the Master Mind principle when he was a young reporter tasked with interviewing America's most successful individuals, one of whom was the formidable steel magnate Andrew Carnegie. During their conversation, Carnegie revealed to Hill that the Master Mind was the primary success principle by which he had made his fortune.[4] Carnegie explained that he took this concept straight from the Bible:

> *In the New Testament, in the story of Christ and his twelve disciples, you'll recall the unusual power the disciples retained after Christ's death through their alliance with him while Christ was himself allied with God. Christ*

7

said to his followers that they could perform even greater things, for he had discovered that the blending of two or more minds in a spirit of harmony with a definite goal gives one contact with the power of the Universal Mind.[5]

As evident in Carnegie's description, the term "Master Mind" refers not only to a group of individuals who ally themselves together in a spirit of harmony to achieve a greater goal, but also to the third mind—the *Master* Mind—that is produced through the association of individual members' minds. Hill explains, "Out of this harmonious blending, the mind creates a third mind that may be appropriated and used by one or all of the individual minds."[6] There are thus two dimensions to the Master Mind: an economic dimension, whereby the members coordinate their knowledge, resources, and efforts to advance their financial or material position; and a psychic dimension, whereby the members organize and direct their thoughts in a spirit of perfect harmony so as to access a higher plane of thinking, one that puts them in direct connection with spiritual forces and sources of knowledge unavailable to the vast majority of individuals. This book will show you how you can appropriate and implement the Master Mind principle so that you can enjoy both aspects of the Master Mind and obtain exponential results on your success journey.

There are two types of Master Mind alliances: alliances formed for purely social or personal reasons, such as those between individuals and their relatives, friends, and/or religious advisors, where no material gain is sought; and alliances formed for business or professional advancement, where the members "have a personal motive of a material or financial nature connected with the object of the alliance."[7] Although this book will focus on the second type of alliance, the principles and activities recommended will, by and large, apply to the maintenance of a successful social or personal Master Mind. In both cases, the most crucial ingredient is harmony: without complete unity of purpose and the total absence of negativity and tension, the Master Mind will not serve the members' aims; to the contrary, disharmony will undercut their efforts. As you read the chapters and work through the action guide, keep at the forefront of your mind the vital nature of harmony for the proper functioning of the Master Mind.

Also, be encouraged—the Master Mind principle is meant to set you at ease and release you from feeling that you have to have, be, and do everything on your own. By virtue of the Master Mind, no individual has to possess *all* the education, experience, character qualities, and skills necessary to achieve their primary goal entirely in their own person. No one need limit their ambition on the account of any self-perceived shortcoming. Anyone—regardless of their location, education, profession, or individual capabilities—can attain their vision of success if they understand and make use of the Master Mind principle. For as Hill tells us, "Knowledge is only potential power. It may become power only when it is organized and directed toward definite ends."[8] The greatest form of education—and consequently, the greatest form of power—is the knowledge of how to use other people's expertise and experience to achieve a definite purpose.

---

*"Knowledge is only potential power.
It may become power only when it is organized
and directed toward definite ends."*
—Napoleon Hill, *Think Your Way to Wealth*

The chapters to come present a roadmap, informed by Napoleon Hill's success philosophy, for creating and leading a Master Mind group. Parts 1 and 2 take you through the process of forming and organizing your alliance, and part 3 offers meeting agendas for twenty-six Master Mind sessions. If your group meets once per week, you can complete the prompts in six months and then go back through them again in the second part of the year to maximize your alliance's consistency and alignment of efforts. Or if you meet every two weeks, the action guide will direct your efforts throughout the entire year.

The power of the Master Mind is electric. In *The Law of Success*, Hill compares it to a series of batteries being connected to a single transmission wire, whereby the power flowing through the line becomes greatly multiplied.[9] By allying yourself with others to create new knowledge, expand personal influence, and identify business solutions, you can leverage the power of the Master Mind to achieve results beyond the capabilities of any one individual.

PART 1

PLANNING AND FORMING
YOUR MASTER MIND GROUP

CHAPTER 1

DETERMINING THE CHIEF AIM
OF YOUR MASTER MIND

Before assembling your Master Mind group, a crucial first step is determining the primary purpose that your alliance will serve—the chief aim that group members will combine their thought power and efforts to achieve. A Master Mind without a definite major purpose will not be able to magnify the group's power of thought and direct it toward constructive ends.

The Master Mind's major purpose must be clear in scope and definite in nature, and it must be established before Master Mind members are selected, because each member needs to have a background that will help achieve it. With a specific chief aim around which the thoughts and actions of members are aligned in a spirit of perfect harmony, the Master Mind can achieve remarkable results. This fact has been borne out by the lives of all truly successful individuals.

Take, for example, Andrew Carnegie, whose Master Mind was organized around the definite major purpose of the making and marketing of steel:

> *Andrew Carnegie stated that he, personally, knew nothing about the technical end of the steel business; moreover, he did not particularly care to know anything about it. The specialized knowledge which he required for the manufacture and marketing of steel, he found available through the individual units of his MASTER MIND GROUP.*[10]

Look, also, at the life and career of Henry Ford, who, despite having less than a sixth-grade education, allied himself with individuals who helped him uncover the secret to mass producing quality automobiles. By associating himself with the great minds of Harvey Firestone, John Burroughs, and Luther Burbank, Ford acquired a power of thought that enabled him to revolutionize the automobile industry. These four men used to go into the woods once a year in order to enjoy some communal reset, meditation, and renewal, and out of the coordination of their individual minds would emerge a Master Mind that would enable them to "tune in" to forces beyond the perception of the average person.

Ford's use of the Master Mind principle became well known when he sued a newspaper for libel after it published a story that referred to him as an "ignorant pacifist." After being interrogated about his knowledge of American history, Ford grew impatient with the defense and exclaimed, "If I should really WANT to answer the foolish question you have just asked, or any of the other questions you have been asking me, let me remind you that I have a row of electric push-buttons on my desk, and by pushing the right button, I can summon to my aid men who can answer ANY question I desire to ask concerning the business to which I am devoting most of my efforts."[11] Ford's remark highlights the power of the Master Mind: one person need not know everything about their major purpose; they simply need to get clear about what their purpose is and then enlist the right individuals to pursue its attainment.

Determine what the primary aim of your Master Mind will be. It could be economic (e.g., obtaining a certain amount of money in life or revenue in business), material (e.g., creating something specific or improving upon something), or psychic (e.g., acquiring power or influence in a specific sector). What is one overarching, desirable, outstanding goal that will govern all your efforts in the group? What final result do you hope to achieve with the assistance of your Master Mind (even if the "final" result is something that can be improved upon over time)? You can—and should—have smaller goals that scaffold toward your definite major purpose, but you must have one larger chief aim toward which you are ultimately striving.

What do you hope to achieve by combining your expertise and experience with the skills and knowledge of other individuals? This is an opportunity to brainstorm your larger goal(s) before distilling your ideas into a definite chief aim.

_____

_____

_____
_____
_____
_____
_____
_____

Refine the answer to the previous question into a concrete sentence that states the definite major purpose of your Master Mind alliance.

_____
_____
_____
_____
_____
_____
_____

What smaller goals will help you accomplish the chief aim of your Master Mind?

_____
_____
_____
_____
_____
_____
_____

CHAPTER 2

CULTIVATING A MAGNETIC PERSONALITY

Not only does a Master Mind alliance require a definite major purpose in order to achieve its aims, but it also must operate in a spirit of perfect harmony. There are many ways to facilitate the creation of this harmony among the minds of individual members: some leaders use force, others employ persuasion, and still others play on members' fear of penalties or desire for rewards. As you can imagine, the use of force, scare tactics, or bribery might encourage members to come together in a spirit of harmony for a short period of time, but their cooperation and unity will not be sustainable. Manipulation never inspires greatness in thought or spirit.

The most effective means of enlisting cooperation from Master Mind members is for the leader to cultivate a magnetic personality "that acts as a nucleus of attraction for other minds."[12] Think, for example, of Napoleon Bonaparte, who attracted other minds to such a great extent that his soldiers would follow him to the death without even flinching. Whether or not you view your alliance's major purpose as a battle to be won, the same principle applies: a magnetic, pleasing personality opens doors, builds bridges, and inspires loyalty, while a coercive personality earns forced, short-lived gains and cuts off access to the spiritual forces available only to the truly collaborative Master Mind. In order to prepare yourself to elicit harmony and cooperation from group members, focus on strengthening the following traits that all magnetic personalities possess.

A magnetic personality "acts as a nucleus of attraction for other minds."

A POSITIVE MENTAL ATTITUDE

The primary trait that people with winning personalities exhibit is a positive mental attitude. All other personality traits listed below are part and parcel of this core character quality. No one wants to be around a negative individual: negativity is contagious; it poisons the environment and produces destructive thought patterns. A positive mental attitude, on the other hand, will attract others to it. People feel uplifted and encouraged by someone with a positive mindset. A positive mental attitude transforms your tone of voice, facial expression, posture, and even the words you use. More than that, it affects every thought you release, building your influence favorably with other individuals. Before you organize your Master Mind alliance, make sure that positivity reigns supreme in your mindset, as it will be key to attracting members and promoting harmony among them.

TOLERANCE

Hill defines tolerance as "an open mind on all subjects toward all people at all times."[13] Intolerant individuals—those who are bigoted, prejudiced, or unable to entertain differences in opinion—create divisiveness, while tolerant individuals create a welcoming environment where others can do their best thinking. Master Mind leaders must never fall prey to intolerant thinking, and they should be careful to select tolerant individuals for members. Fear, ignorance, and superstition grow out of—and feed—intolerance, and these qualities will cause a Master Mind alliance to quickly collapse, or worse—act in harmful ways.

A KEEN SENSE OF JUSTICE AND HONESTY

Individuals with a magnetic personality live according to a strong moral compass. They have taken time to define their non-negotiable personal values, and they align all their actions with these values. They regularly engage in self-reflection to ensure that their path accords with their values and purpose and that their actions are not violating the rights of another individual. They have a sound and dependable character, for they will always do what is right simply because it is right, not because they will receive an immediate advantage or a reward.

FLEXIBILITY

In order to have a winning personality, you must be able to adapt to change without losing your composure. Moreover, you must be willing to adapt your personality to connect with various individuals. "A person with a flexible disposition must be something like a chameleon, able to quickly change color to harmonize with the environment."[14] According to Andrew Carnegie, Charles Schwab became one of America's greatest salesmen by cultivating this personality trait: "He could get down on the ground and play a game of marbles with a group of boys and then get up and walk into his office and be ready to enter a Master Mind meeting where he was called on to make decisions involving millions of dollars."[15] Individuals with a pleasing personality are versatile: they have basic knowledge of many subjects and feel comfortable conversing on a myriad of topics in various situations. Never become so rigid in your mentality that you cannot relate to a wide variety of people or adjust to changing circumstances.

SELF-DISCIPLINE

The next quality exhibited by people with magnetic personalities is self-discipline, which includes the character traits of temperance, patience, and controlled temper. Temperance involves moderation and self-restraint in all things. Excess in anything—eating, drinking, sex, or other activities—will likely destroy personal magnetism. Another application of self-discipline that is crucial for developing a dynamic character is patience, which Hill defines as "calm and uncomplaining endurance under pain or provocation and a quiet perseverance."[16] Train yourself to avoid acting impetuously, including when your ire is aroused. A controlled temper, or the ability to harness emotion and direct it toward constructive ends, is key to maintaining influence among those in your circle.

DECISIVENESS

Although rashness detracts from personal magnetism, the ability to make quick and firm decisions contributes to it. This is not a contradiction: the individual with a pleasing personality does not act in the heat of the moment because he or she is overwhelmed with emotion or influenced by the opinions of others; rather, that person makes timely decisions based on logic and sound counsel. And once a decision is made, the individual will not change it because of a whim or fancy. Those with strength of presence are quick to make a decision and slow to change it.

EFFECTIVE COMMUNICATION

There are many elements that contribute to effective communication. The first is the ability to voice emotion without losing control of it. If your voice can resonate strongly, modulate its tone to create a dramatic effect, and convey the emotion of the content in a poised way, it will draw people toward you and inspire them to act. The effective communicator also knows how to speak assertively, demonstrating confidence in the topic on which he or she is conversing. In order to do this, you must be thoroughly knowledgeable on the subject.

Smiling while talking and listening also goes a long way toward building favor with others. When a person smiles, we recognize that smile to be indicative of a positive mental attitude, and so we are drawn to that individual in the hope of being uplifted ourselves.

Tactfulness is another factor that contributes to effective communication. The person who knows how to do and say the right thing at the right time will always attract others. On the other hand, the person who says the wrong thing at the wrong time, or even the right thing at the wrong time, will end up causing unintended offense and harming potential business or personal relationships.

Of course, none of these traits would be possible in the absence of the ability to use words appropriately. Therefore, be careful to convey your exact meaning by using clear, precise language.

HUMILITY

Arrogance and egotism push people away from us, whereas humility of heart attracts people to us. Humility arises from gratitude for the material possessions we already have and a recognition of the dignity and value of every individual. When we comprehend that our personal achievements or possessions do not make us superior to others, but rather enable us to serve others, then we open the door to collaboration of the highest form.

SENSE OF HUMOR

Human beings like to laugh; we like to enjoy our pursuits. That means in order to magnetize our personality, we need to have a sense of humor, first and foremost about ourselves and next about the events occurring around us. Humor supports our resilience and flexibility because we can be at ease as we adjust to life's changing circumstances. It boosts our tolerance, as we learn to take everything with a grain of salt. It improves our overall physical and mental health. Hill tells us that "the person who cannot relax and live at the proper time is to be pitied, missing the better portion of life's benefits no matter other assets. We need some method of escape from our routine occupation, enabling us a break in the monotony, serving as a tonic for the maintenance of sound physical health."[17] Smile, laugh, and avoid taking yourself too seriously—this will benefit your contentment and draw others toward you.

POISE AND APPROPRIATE SELF-PRESENTATION

Individuals with personal magnetism are patient; they quietly persevere and remain poised regardless of the challenges they face or the provocations they receive from others. They present themselves with care as to the impression they will make, attending to expectations for appropriate dress. They shake hands in a way that conveys enthusiasm and congeniality. Good showmanship similarly boosts personal magnetism: when we display our enthusiasm for what we are doing in a way that excites others, we invite buy-in to our endeavors. Another related trait is the willingness to champion others—their ideas and their contributions—which makes the individual celebrating others' positive qualities just as appealing as the recipients of the praise.

FONDNESS FOR OTHERS

At a very basic level, we must exhibit a fondness for others. People can quickly discern whether an individual has a general dislike for others, and when this becomes apparent, ill favor will soon follow. Hill confirms that "it's inevitable that people who like others will be liked themselves, since everyone picks up on attitudes and acts on them."[18] People will meet your expectations for their behavior, so go through your day with the assumption that others are pleasant, enjoyable, and helpful, and that will be your experience with them.

If you can cultivate these traits and move through your day-to-day life with a pleasing personality, then you will enhance your ability to form a strong Master Mind alliance. And the Master Mind is the ultimate magnetic personality that attracts to you the favor, support, and ideas of other individuals.

How do you plan to attract the right individuals to your Master Mind and maintain their unity of purpose?

_____

_____

_____

_____

_____

What qualities of a magnetic personality do you already possess?

_____

_____

_____

_____

_____

Which qualities do you need to develop or strengthen?

_____

_____

_____

_____

_____

Hill recommends using the sixth sense, also known as the creative imagination, to enhance one's character through what he terms "Invisible Counselors." This process involves creating an imaginary Master Mind of both living and dead individuals who possess the character traits you desire with whom you meet regularly in deep visualization sessions.

First, for every quality in which you identified yourself as being deficient, name 2–3 individuals, either living or dead, who possess that trait in abundance.

TRAIT ONE: **EXEMPLARS OF THAT TRAIT:**

_____   _____

                                _____

                                _____

TRAIT TWO: **EXEMPLARS OF THAT TRAIT:**

_____   _____

                                _____

                                _____

TRAIT THREE: **EXEMPLARS OF THAT TRAIT:**

_____   _____

                                _____

                                _____

TRAIT FOUR: **EXEMPLARS OF THAT TRAIT:**

_____   _____

                                _____

                                _____

(Continue this exercise on a separate sheet of paper if you would like to strengthen additional traits.)

For each trait, choose one individual who epitomizes that trait; indicate your choice by circling their name.

Write your group of Invisible Counselors below. Schedule a session with them for a time when you can have a quiet, undisturbed environment. When it is time, call the meeting to order and, one by one, ask each individual to share with you their secret for developing the desired trait. Insist that they reveal their methods and philosophy to you. Record any insights that arise from your Invisible Counselor meetings below.

_____

_____

_____

_____

_____

_____

_____

_____

_____

_____

_____

_____

_____

_____

_____

_____

_____

_____

_____

_____

_____

CHAPTER 3

SELECTING AND INVITING
MASTER MIND MEMBERS

Andrew Carnegie, who amassed a billion-dollar steel empire, swore by the Master Mind principle for its ability to magnify an individual's capacity for achievement. But he was successful at harnessing the power of the Master Mind only because he was a great "picker of men." He knew how to find, surround himself with, and tap the intelligence of the right individuals. In order to get the most out of your Master Mind alliance, you need to ensure that you select the best individuals for your purposes.

It is typical for Master Mind alliances to be formed between individuals who did not know each other prior to their involvement with the group. As the originator of the Master Mind group, you might reach out to specific people whom you know will contribute the right expertise or experience, or you might choose to issue a call for members. If you pursue the latter option, you should create one or more position descriptions—essentially, job ads for the type(s) of individual(s) for whom you are searching to fill in the group's knowledge or influence gaps. Interested parties will then communicate their interest to you with details about how they meet the stated needs of the group, and you will select from the available applicants.

During this stage, you should also consider whether there are certain requirements you will establish for membership, such as a specific salary level, industry, following/network, etc. Limit your applicants by these characteristics *only* if you are certain these qualifications are absolutely necessary to the success of the group. Remember, a diversity of experiences, perspectives, and positions can greatly contribute to the group's creative power.

After you have established the definite major purpose of your Master Mind alliance and identified potential members, you should measure each candidate against the following non-negotiable requirements:

- They possess a positive mental attitude.
- They have the background, traits, skills, and/or connections to contribute purposefully to the achievement of the alliance's definite major purpose.
- They do not treat failure as something that is definite and irreversible but rather as a lesson which, if learned, can reveal a seed of opportunity.
- They will harmonize with the other individuals in the group.

Let's explore each qualification in turn.

A POSITIVE MENTAL ATTITUDE

Nothing will poison a group faster than an individual with a negative mental attitude. For this reason, it is crucial that you ensure each member possesses a positive mindset. They should have a well-developed success consciousness; in other words, they have a firm belief in their ability to achieve their goals. This success consciousness will transfer to the Master Mind, where the individual will be certain of the alliance's ultimate success in attaining its definite chief aim.

THE RIGHT BACKGROUND AND QUALITIES TO SUPPORT THE ALLIANCE'S MAJOR PURPOSE

Next, a candidate for your Master Mind alliance should possess some experience, trait, skill, connection, or influence that will benefit the group's ability to achieve its definite major purpose. Hill enjoins the Master Mind leader to "choose individual members whose education, experience, and influence will provide the greatest value in achieving your purpose."[19] He further explains:

> Each member of the alliance should make a distinctive and unique contribution to complete the picture. Don't choose people mainly because you know them and like them; you should be guided in your choice by what you need. If you need money to finance the deal, choose a person who has money to invest. You must find this person and cultivate a willingness to cooperate with you.[20]

26

It is worth underscoring Hill's warning against choosing individuals merely because you like or respect them. In a similar vein, you will want to avoid selecting only those individuals who agree wholesale with your attitudes and beliefs. While you will want to ensure that every potential member has a positive mental attitude, a resilience that enables them to withstand temporary defeat, along with tolerance and other harmony-promoting characteristics, you do not want to construct an echo chamber with a group of yes-men and yes-women. Having members with diverse experiences, knowledge, beliefs, and qualities will greatly benefit your Master Mind, as it will lead to more creative thinking, better planning, and stronger solutions. Focus on the skills, expertise, and connections you need to achieve your chief aim.

AN UNWILLINGNESS TO ACCEPT FAILURE AS FINAL

Ideal Master Mind members do not fold at the first sign of defeat. They do not give up when challenges arise. Instead, they brace themselves to withstand adversity, recognizing that all defeat—with the right mindset—is temporary. Moreover, they appreciate the benefits that can come from adversity and live according to Hill's dictum that "every failure brings with it the seed of an equivalent advantage."[21]

A PROCLIVITY FOR HARMONIOUS RELATIONS

Finally, any potential Master Mind member should excel at maintaining harmony within a group. They should be open-minded and tolerant of different beliefs. They should not be given to gossip or slander—even about individuals who rightfully deserve criticism. Any sign that a Master Mind candidate creates or fuels tension, or that he or she offends or undercuts others, should be taken as evidence not to include that individual in your alliance. For the Master Mind that lacks harmony will not generate constructive results and will eventually fall apart.

After you have measured each potential Master Mind member against the above qualifications and narrowed down your list to a small group of individuals— Hill recommends six to seven members to start—it is time to invite those you selected to participate in your alliance.

Approach each person individually, asking them to meet with you to discuss how you can support each other to achieve a greater goal. In the one-on-one session, ask the person questions that draw out what their definite major purpose in life is, and then collaboratively determine how it might be served by achieving the definite chief aim you have established for the Master Mind alliance. Use this meeting to gather insight about what motivates the individual. (We will explore how to use motives to keep the Master Mind alliance active and harmonious in chapter 5.)

Ensure the watchword of the alliance remains: "Definiteness of Purpose backed by perfect harmony and consistent action."

When the moment feels right, ask the individual if they would like to join your Master Mind alliance to obtain the specific chief aim you have set for the group. Verify that they would commit to attaining that purpose and to maintaining harmony within the alliance at all costs. But do not try to sell each person on the merits of your Master Mind group. If they are the right individual, they will have the right attitude about joining the group.

Treat your Master Mind alliance like a dynamic group that must be assessed and restructured according to its needs. If a member begins spreading negativity in the group or otherwise disturbs the group's harmony, revoke that individual's membership and replace them with someone who will contribute more positively to the alliance. Never get so set in your ways or so complacent that you are unable to see when the group's thought power is being diminished by a disharmonious member. Ensure the watchword of the alliance remains: *"Definiteness of Purpose backed by perfect harmony and consistent action."*[22]

On the next page, identify the experience, expertise (specialized knowledge), skills, qualities, connections, and influence you need to achieve the definite major purpose of your Master Mind alliance.

EXPERIENCE

**EXPERTISE
(SPECIALIZED KNOWLEDGE)**

SKILLS

QUALITIES

CONNECTIONS

INFLUENCE

For every need listed on page 29, identify an individual (someone who is alive and with whom you can connect) who would fulfill it.

_____

_____

_____

_____

_____

_____

_____

_____

_____

_____

_____

_____

Evaluate each potential Master Mind member against the four requirements given in this chapter. _As a reminder, these are: (1) a positive mental attitude; (2) background, traits, skills, and/or connections that would contribute purposefully to the achievement of the alliance's definite major purpose; (3) an unwillingness to accept failure as final; and (4) the ability to maintain harmonious relations._

_____

_____

_____

_____

_____

_____

_____

_____

_____

_____

_____

_____

_____

_____

_____

_____

_____

_____

_____

_____

_____

_____

Based on the assessment in the previous exercise, compose a list of the individuals you would like to invite to participate in your Master Mind alliance. Try to keep your initial list to 6–7 individuals.

1.

2.

3.

4.

5.

6.

7.

Invite each person using the method described at the end of this chapter. Record notes about what you learn regarding their primary aim, smaller goals, motives, interests, and more.

_____

_____

_____

_____

_____

_____

_____

_____

_____

_____

_____

_____

_____

_____

_____

_____

_____

_____

_____

_____

_____

After each candidate responds to your invitation, provide the final list of your Master Mind members below.

MY MASTER MIND GROUP

1.

2.

3.

4.

5.

6.

7.

PART 2

MANAGING YOUR MASTER MIND GROUP

CHAPTER 4

ORGANIZING YOUR MASTER MIND MEETINGS

Now that you have formed your Master Mind group, it is crucial that you establish a plan for the alliance's meetings. Maintaining a regular rhythm is essential for the success of your group. For as Hill suggests, "To be effective, a Master Mind alliance must be active."[23]

First, determine how often your group will meet: every two weeks, weekly, or twice per week are good options. Poll members to determine their availability. Based on the results, establish a schedule of the day(s) and time(s) when you will meet as a group. Ideally, the schedule should remain consistent—for example, every Tuesday from 5:30 to 6:30 p.m. Dedicate at least one hour to every session. The more you can build a natural rhythm into your meetings, the more likely the members will be to commit to regular attendance. Your sessions should occur in person or via a video call, as it is important to be able to be in the presence, virtual or otherwise, of your group members.

Once you have established your meeting schedule and are ready for your first session, task members with creating a charter for your alliance. This charter should specify:

- The group's leadership
- Roles assigned to specific members (e.g., peacekeeper, minute taker, discussion leader, etc.)
- Strengths and assets that members bring to the group
- The alliance's major purpose (what success looks like for the group)
- Smaller goals or milestones that have already been identified as being necessary to support the achievement of the group's major purpose
- The timeline for the achievement of major/minor goals
- The group's meeting schedule

- An agreement to attend consistently and policies for how to handle poor attendance
- Expectations for member participation (with special attention to maintaining harmony)
- Obstacles or challenges that can be identified at the outset and how the group will handle them

After drawing up a document containing all of this information, each group member should sign the master copy, which should then be reproduced and given to every member for their reference. Every person needs to be totally aligned with the purpose of the Master Mind, its schedule, and its procedures. They need to be 100 percent committed to attending consistently, for the alliance will not be able to harness the power of the Master Mind without all of its members combining their thought power to generate better ideas and stronger plans.

Note: The action guide contained in part 3 of this book provides specific prompts for creating a Master Mind charter and engaging in other activities that will support your group's pursuit of its major purpose.

Once the Master Mind charter has been established, members should spend time analyzing the alliance's major purpose and identifying what is needed for its attainment. Ask questions like:

- What steps need to be taken in order to achieve our major goal by the established date?
- What material resources will we need to complete each of those steps?
- What intangible resources (specialized knowledge, influence, access to certain individuals, etc.) are necessary to accomplish our aims?
- Whose expertise, connections, influence, and/or experience will help us accomplish each of those steps?
- What challenges can we anticipate, and how can we be proactive about handling them effectively?

Outlining a general plan for the attainment of the alliance's major goal early on in your meetings will help focus your sessions and create space for refining your plans, making them more concrete, acting on them, and finding ways to be flexible when new plans need to be generated.

Individual sessions should follow set agendas, samples of which are provided in part 3 of this book. However, at the beginning of every meeting, it is a good idea to help the group get in the flow by engaging in mental and social exercises. Each sample agenda in this book opens with a potential "flow activity." You should establish a specific amount of time to engage in this flow activity each meeting and then move the group to order when that time has elapsed. Once the time for the icebreaker has concluded, be sure to focus the group on the Master Mind activities planned for that day, as you will not want to make the mistake of treating your alliance like a social club.

Sometimes the flow of everyone's ideas will be so powerful that the meeting will run over its allotted time. Don't be afraid to lean into this flow when it happens, because innovation doesn't follow a set schedule. However, do not allow every meeting to run late. Respect members' other commitments—to their job, to their family, to their wellness, etc.—by ending meetings punctually. By treating every meeting with care and consistency, it will enable the alliance to produce high-level thoughts and remain motivated to act on the group's plans.

How often will the group meet (monthly, biweekly, weekly, or twice per week)? And how long? Explain your rationale for these decisions.

_____

_____

_____

_____

_____

_____

_____

Will the group meet in person or virtually by video call? Explain your rationale for this choice.

_____

_____

_____

_____

Do you need to add any other components (other than those mentioned above) to your Master Mind charter?

_____

_____

_____

_____

What roles would you like to establish for certain members of your Master Mind (e.g., timekeeper, peacekeeper, minute taker, decision maker, discussion leader, etc.)?

_____

_____

_____

_____

How would you prefer to handle issues with member attendance?

_____

_____

_____

_____

Are there additional questions you would like your Master Mind members to address when identifying what is needed for the attainment of your group's major purpose?

_____

_____

_____

_____

_____

_____

CHAPTER 5

MAINTAINING HARMONY AMONG MEMBERS

Without harmony, a Master Mind alliance is merely a group of individuals who meet regularly; it is not a true Master Mind. As Hill suggests, "Harmony is the nucleus around which the state of mind known as 'Master Mind' must be developed. Without this element of harmony, there can be no 'Master Mind,' a truth that cannot be repeated too often."[24] That is why whenever he defines "Master Mind," Hill emphasizes the necessity of harmony. For example:

> *"a mind that grows out of the blending and coordination of two or more minds IN A SPIRIT OF PERFECT HARMONY."*[25]

> *"an alliance of two or more people working in harmony—perfect harmony—with a positive mental attitude for the attainment of a definite end."*[26]

Harmony is essential because, Hill explains, "the major strength of such an alliance consists in the perfect meeting of the minds of all our members. Jealousy, envy, or friction, as well as a lagging of interest on the part of any member, will bring almost certain defeat."[27] All groups experience friction, so how can you protect your Master Mind from this natural tendency?

IMPLEMENT A MOTIVE STRUCTURE

It is the leader's responsibility to ensure that harmony prevails among members and that members are taking action consistently toward the group's definite major purpose. If the leader has a magnetic personality, that will promote harmony within the group, as his or her charisma will transfer to group members and keep them motivated. In addition to cultivating a magnetic personality, the leader can foster harmony through the intelligent use of motives. Every member should have a clear motive for participating in the alliance. Hill cautions:

There must be a motive. You can have no Master Mind alliance without every individual member always having a motive. You must be getting something out of it. You can't form a Master Mind alliance and use the brains, and the experience, and the friendship, and the love and affection, and maybe even the capital of another person without getting something back from it. Even though someone may be willing to give it for a time, don't accept it. Don't accept anything from anybody unless you are giving something of an equivalent value in return in one way or another.[28]

Therefore, the leader must "determine what appropriate benefit each member may receive in return for his or her cooperation in the alliance, and see that each one gets it."[29]

The members of your Master Mind might have any number of different motives that would incite them to act in the group's favor, but these individual desires will fall under the banner of one or more of what Hill terms the "nine basic motives":

1. The desire for sex expression and love
2. The desire for physical food
3. The desire for spiritual, mental, and physical self-expression
4. The desire for perpetuation of life after death
5. The desire for power over others
6. The desire for material wealth
7. The desire for knowledge
8. The desire to imitate others
9. The desire to excel over others

All voluntary physical action is inspired by one or more of these nine motives. When you were forming your Master Mind group, you should have surveyed potential members to determine what interests them, what excites them, what inspires them, and what motivates them. Using that knowledge, you should create a "Motive Map" to identify the best motives to use to keep every member invested in attaining the group's larger purpose. A template for this exercise is provided at the end of this chapter. Below are the steps:

1. Compile a list of group members' individual motives for participating in the alliance.
2. Organize them into categories according to the nine basic motives.
3. Pinpoint several larger motives that will inspire most—if not all—of the members to take action according to your Master Mind's major purpose.

Once you have mapped out the motives that can be employed to maintain group harmony, don't sit on the information! Ensure that members are enjoying benefits connected to their motives. For example, if a Master Mind member is primarily motivated by a desire to gain knowledge, then occasionally assign an article, chapter, or even an entire book to members to read on their own time, and then build discussion time into your Master Mind meetings. Make sure that all of the readings are relevant to the object of your Master Mind: while they do not need to be focused on the exact topic of your purpose, they should contribute to its attainment. That is, if your Master Mind was formed to build an online course offering in customer service training, you could circulate articles, chapters, and books not only on customer service, but also on leadership, empathy, and communication. The bottom line is, for members to remain engaged, positive, and active, they must see a payoff for their efforts—and not only when group goals are met, but also (and especially) in the thick of the work. Get creative about ways to inspire members: combine words of encouragement with individual incentives and group activities.

REMOVE NEGATIVE INFLUENCES

In addition to blending a magnetic personality with an effective motive structure, the Master Mind leader must regularly analyze the atmosphere of the group and weed out any negative influences that are present. The inability or unwillingness to identify and address destructive attitudes, thoughts, and actions within the group is a surefire way to ensure the failure of your group. Don't undercut your group's success because you dislike confrontation or are too caught up in the creative elements of the Master Mind to notice when a toxic influence is poisoning the group.

At least every week, the leader should perform a harmony check on the group, a template for which is provided at the end of this chapter. Assess the following dynamics of your alliance:

- What is going really well in the group right now? What is producing harmony?
  - How can you build more of what is working into your Master Mind meetings?
- What is the current emotional atmosphere of the group? Are there any points of tension or negative emotions present?
  - What might be causing these points of tension?
  - How can you eliminate them?
  - Do any members need to be replaced?
  - Who might you add to your group to improve the harmony?

Harmony is not a one-time achievement to be celebrated but rather an ongoing commitment to live out.

Determine what is supporting harmonious relations in the group, and make sure you are intentional about injecting those elements into the meetings. Analyze what is limiting the group's ability to operate without discord, jealousy, or apathy, and address it immediately. Possible sources of negativity might include:

- One or more members feeling discouraged about the alliance's progress toward its major goal
- One or more members feeling jealous about how another member is being treated
- One or more members feeling bitter about the amount of effort they are contributing relative to other group members
- One or more members bringing outside opinions into the group rather than relying on their own informed thoughts and the counsel of other members
- One or more members allowing external fears or misinformation to penetrate the group

Once you have identified the reasons for disharmony within your Master Mind, create a plan for uprooting the source(s). Do not allow time to strengthen the hold that negativity has over your group. If you have to remove members from your group, do it without hesitation. Every member in that group has signed a charter agreeing to maintain harmony; the failure to support harmonious relations is a violation of your charter and subject to the consequence upon which group members have agreed.

Harmony has to be cultivated with intentionality—not once, not twice, but day by day and week by week. It is not a one-time achievement to be celebrated but rather an ongoing commitment to live out. Without it, a group is a Master Mind in name only, for it will not access the higher plane of thinking available to the psychic "third mind" generated by a harmonious group actively working to achieve a definite major purpose.

Create a Motive Map to visualize the incentives you can use to ensure Master Mind members remain committed to attaining the group's larger purpose.

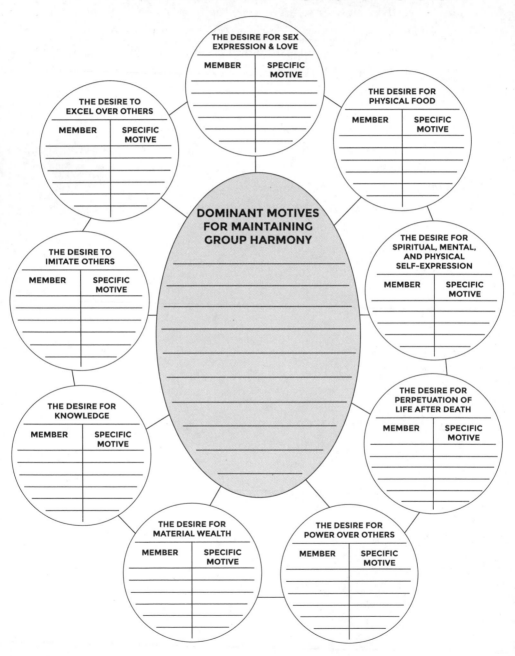

Based on your Motive Map, list actions, incentives, and activities you can offer individual members and the group as a whole to keep them inspired and committed.

INDIVIDUAL OFFERINGS	GROUP OFFERINGS

Conduct a "harmony check" in your group regularly—at least once per week. Use the boxes below to strategize ways for improving the harmony in your group. Continue this exercise, if need be, in a separate notebook or journal.

HARMONY CHECK #1		Date:
What is going really well in the group right now? What is producing harmony?		
How can you build more of what is working into your Master Mind meetings?		
What is the current emotional atmosphere of the group? Are there any points of tension or negative emotions present?		
What might be causing these points of tension?		
How can you eliminate them?		
Do any members need to be replaced? Who might you add?		

HARMONY CHECK #2	Date:
What is going really well in the group right now? What is producing harmony?	
How can you build more of what is working into your Master Mind meetings?	
What is the current emotional atmosphere of the group? Are there any points of tension or negative emotions present?	
What might be causing these points of tension?	
How can you eliminate them?	
Do any members need to be replaced? Who might you add?	

HARMONY CHECK #3	Date:
What is going really well in the group right now? What is producing harmony?	
How can you build more of what is working into your Master Mind meetings?	
What is the current emotional atmosphere of the group? Are there any points of tension or negative emotions present?	
What might be causing these points of tension?	
How can you eliminate them?	
Do any members need to be replaced? Who might you add?	

HARMONY CHECK #4	Date:
What is going really well in the group right now? What is producing harmony?	
How can you build more of what is working into your Master Mind meetings?	
What is the current emotional atmosphere of the group? Are there any points of tension or negative emotions present?	
What might be causing these points of tension?	
How can you eliminate them?	
Do any members need to be replaced? Who might you add?	

CHAPTER 6

TRANSLATING GROUP INSIGHT INTO ACTION

The final step of managing a Master Mind alliance is establishing a definite plan through which each member will contribute something specific toward the achievement of the alliance's major goal. Without a plan, Hill tells us, a Master Mind group cannot hope to achieve anything of substance:

> *Every well-built house started in the form of a definite purpose plus a definite plan, in the nature of a set of blueprints. Imagine what would happen if one tried to build a house by the haphazard method, without plans. Workmen would be in each other's way, building material would be piled all over the lot before the foundation was completed, and everybody on the job would have a different notion as to how the house ought to be built. Result: chaos and misunderstandings and cost that would be prohibitive.*[30]

Your plan should be generated from the coordination of members' minds during meetings, refined through continuous discussion, and put into action week by week. Below are the steps for brainstorming ideas and then translating them into action.

DEFINE THE OPPORTUNITY

How you frame the question of how to accomplish your ultimate goal matters just as much as the efforts you undertake to answer it. Even if you are facing a great difficulty, it is best to approach your challenge not as a problem or issue, but as an opportunity waiting to be realized.

Next, get specific about what you are looking to do. What solution are you attempting to generate? Together with your group, list all the known details about the potential opportunity. Use a flip chart, whiteboard, or other large, blank canvas to record every piece of information that members share.

Then, establish connections between ideas: draw lines or arrows between similar or process-related items, circle important concepts, number items as needed—or, using another writing space, create a mind map to organize the information. The goal of this step is to establish in very clear terms the parameters of the group's definite major purpose.

DETERMINE WHAT INFORMATION IS NECESSARY

Even with all the members' expertise and skills, it is likely that additional information will be required to fully understand the opportunity and the best means of realizing it. Survey the conceptual diagram you completed in the last step:

- What elements should be researched to better ascertain how they will contribute to the Master Mind's larger goal?
- Where can you obtain this specialized knowledge?
- Whom should be tasked with locating it?
- How can you verify that your findings are both accurate and relevant to your purpose?

Assign research tasks to members and designate specific Master Mind meetings for the evaluation of the information that is presented. From this step you should emerge with a more developed picture of the various components necessary to achieve the group's larger goal.

IDENTIFY WHAT RESOURCES AND ACTIONS ARE REQUIRED

Once you have a clearer picture of all the elements necessary to attain your definite chief aim, determine what resources and action steps you will need to take. At this point, you are not necessarily trying to organize the steps into a specific order. You are not creating a plan or timeline. You are merely trying to identify everything you will need to accomplish your purpose. As a group, answer the following questions:

- How can we break down larger goals into smaller ones?
- What specific actions will be required to realize these smaller goals?

- How long can we reasonably expect each step to take?
- What resources (financial, material, people, technological, etc.) are needed to achieve these smaller goals?
- How can we obtain these resources? Who will be responsible for attaining and managing each necessary resource?
- When can these resources be obtained?

Write a list of everything you need and determine the dates by which you will procure the required resources.

CREATE A WORKING DRAFT OF YOUR PLAN

With your opportunity clearly defined and the various components and necessary resources mapped out, it is time to collectively brainstorm a provisional plan to achieve your group's major purpose. Do not let fears or concerns impede your ideation. Master Mind alliances are more readily able to activate the creative imagination, what Hill terms "the sixth sense," and need to be free of judgment, fear, and bias in order to enjoy its benefits. Demand that the universe offer you a plan for accomplishing your larger goal by the deadline you have established. Raise the vibration of your collective thoughts by injecting them with definiteness of purpose, desire, and faith in the certainty of a successful outcome.

As you outline your plan, ensure that it has definite steps whose success can be verified before moving on. Pinpoint a deadline by which each step should be completed. Decide how you will define success for each step and what you will do when a step has not been completed satisfactorily. Determine what individuals and the group as a whole are willing to give in return for the completion of each step. Assign each step a manager—a Master Mind member who is ultimately responsible for coordinating its progress and ensuring its timely completion. By the end of this planning phase, you should have a working draft of your plan that can be further discussed and refined within the group.

USE A SWOT ANALYSIS TO REFINE YOUR PLAN

SWOT analyses (strengths, weaknesses, opportunities, and threats analyses) are helpful tools used by organizations to evaluate the soundness of a particular business strategy or decision. They are also useful for refining the working draft of your plan. As a group, determine:

- **What are the strengths of our proposed plan?** How is it based on solid research and analysis? How is it the best use of our resources? How does it offer a reasonable timeline for completion that also challenges us? How is it unique? What benefits will it produce that will support the attainment of our major goal? How will it serve others?
- **What are the weaknesses of our provisional plan?** Have we made any assumptions that could undercut our progress? How are resources being wasted or at least not maximized? Do we lack necessary resources and could we struggle to obtain them? Do any timelines need to be adjusted? Are there any internal or external factors for which we did not account? Are any of the steps too vague?
- **What opportunities will be created by this plan?** What new options will result as we complete each step? What opportunities can we take advantage of to ensure our ultimate success?
- **What threats might thwart our progress?** What threats, both internal and external to the group, might cause us to lose momentum? Are we competing with anyone, and if so, might they cause any interference? What risks are involved?

Based on your evaluation of the plan, refine its elements until you produce a more definite plan that is less likely to fail when adversity strikes.

PUT YOUR PLAN INTO ACTION

Now that you have refined your plan and rendered it more concrete, it is time for the most important planning step—putting it into action. Begin at once to implement the plan, whether you are ready or not. Do not wait until the time seems right to act on it. There will always be some reason that you could delay a little longer, but every day you wait is another day that you are getting further from your definite major purpose—and another day you are losing self-confidence and the definiteness of purpose necessary to achieve success. Heed Andrew Carnegie's advice to Napoleon Hill:

Once formed, a Master Mind group must become and remain active to be effective. The group must move on a definite plan, at a definite time, toward a definite end. Indecision, inaction, and delay will destroy the usefulness of the entire group. Plus, the best way to keep the members in harmony is through continuous work.[31]

Do not get stuck worrying about whether your plan is the best one. As Hill reveals, "The major difference between a sound and an unsound plan is that the sound plan, if definitely applied, may be carried out more quickly than an unsound plan."[32] In other words, if you cannot be perfectly right in your plan, at least be definite in your application of it—if you persist through temporary defeat, you will accomplish your goals, regardless of whether your plan was sound.

If you cannot be perfectly right in your plan, at least be definite in your application of it.

Keep your plan between you and your Master Mind group; do not announce your intentions to those outside your alliance. In *Think and Grow Rich*, Hill underscores the importance of acting on your plan before bragging about it to others: "TELL THE WORLD WHAT YOU INTEND TO DO, BUT FIRST SHOW IT."[33] If you tell people outside of your Master Mind alliance about your plan, they might criticize or question you, or they could take your idea and act on it themselves; both responses are detrimental to your success.

As each Master Mind member holds the plan in their mind and takes steps to fulfill it, the third mind formed in the harmonious union will take over the plan and coordinate with Infinite Intelligence to accelerate the group's progress. Remember: the most important aspects of creating and implementing a plan within the context of a Master Mind group are (1) aligning your (positive) thoughts about the certainty of your plan's ultimate success, even before you have created one; and (2) acting on your plan consistently until your definite chief aim has been attained.

On your own, define the opportunity that you are trying to realize through the attainment of your definite major purpose.

_____

_____

_____

_____

_____

_____

What information or specialized knowledge will be necessary to take advantage of that opportunity? Who among your group members possesses this knowledge? What additional information will have to be gathered through research?

_____

_____

_____

_____

_____

_____

What resources (financial, material, people, technological, etc.) will be required to reach your major goal? Which ones are already available to you? Which ones will you need to obtain?

_____

_____

_____

_____

_____

_____

What can you do to ensure that you and the other Master Mind members remain active in your attempts to achieve the group's larger purpose?

_____

_____

_____

_____

_____

_____

PART 3

SAMPLE MASTER MIND MEETING AGENDAS

ESTABLISHING PROCESSES

TODAY'S OUTCOME

Create a Master Mind charter that all group members sign.

FLOW ACTIVITY

Ask members to share their answers to the following questions:
- What are you hoping to gain from participating in this Master Mind?
- What do you do to ensure you remain motivated and accountable to your commitments in life and business?

MEETING AGENDA

1. Create a charter for your Master Mind group. Include the following information:
   - The group's leadership
   - Roles assigned to specific members (e.g., peacekeeper, minute taker, discussion leader etc.)
   - Strengths and assets that members bring to the group
   - The alliance's major purpose (what success looks like for the group)
   - Smaller goals or milestones that have already been identified as being necessary to support the achievement of the group's major purpose
   - The timeline for the achievement of major/minor goals
   - The group's meeting schedule
   - An agreement to attend consistently and policies for how to handle poor attendance
   - Expectations for member participation (with special attention to maintaining harmony)
   - Obstacles or challenges that can be identified at the outset and how the group will handle them

2. Once the charter has been finalized, ask every member to sign it.

ACTION ITEMS

- Photocopy your Master Mind charter and distribute it to all members.
- Every member should create a list of their motives for participating in the Master Mind. Next to every motive, they should write one thing they can do to stay committed to this incentive when they are feeling uninspired.

Notes

ANALYZING YOUR OPPORTUNITY

TODAY'S OUTCOME

Explore the opportunities inherent within
your Master Mind's definite major purpose.

FLOW ACTIVITY

Ask members to visualize themselves enjoying what they believe is the highest form of success. Acknowledge that every person in the room (or on the screen) might have a different definition of success and that is completely fine—they should personalize this vision according to their dreams. Coach members to visualize as many details as possible: *Where are you? Whom are you with? What is everyone wearing? What is your facial expression? What emotions can you feel in that space? What are you doing? What are others doing? Can you hear, taste, smell, see, or feel anything additional in this space? What do those sensory impressions tell you about your experience of success?*

Give everyone five minutes to build out the picture in their minds, and then ask members to share specific details from their exercise. You might choose to level up the discussion by asking members to share something that surprised them about their mental imagery.

MEETING AGENDA

1. Build out in great detail the definite major purpose of your Master Mind by working together to answer the following questions:
   - What solution are you attempting to generate?
     - Are you trying to solve a specific problem?
     - Are you trying to provide a new service or product?
     - Are you attempting to acquire or create a specific form of knowledge?

- What potential benefits will result from the attainment of this purpose?
  - What value are you adding?
  - Who will directly benefit from your efforts?
  - Who will indirectly benefit from your efforts?
  - What are the short- and long-term opportunities that will arise?

ACTION ITEMS

- Save the flip chart page or the whiteboard from this brainstorming session, or transfer the ideas to a piece of paper, and bring this to your next Master Mind session.
- Ask every member to draft a statement of the group's definite major purpose to bring to the next meeting.

Notes

DEFINING YOUR MAJOR PURPOSE

TODAY'S OUTCOME

Define in detail the definite major purpose of your Master Mind.

FLOW ACTIVITY

If everyone in the group could be a superhero, what would their special ability be (and why)? Whom would they serve with that power (and why)? What would be their kryptonite (the one thing that would diminish their powers), and why?

MEETING AGENDA

1. Before the meeting commences, display the flip chart page or whiteboard from the last Master Mind session—or transfer the notes you recorded to a large piece of paper or whiteboard—so that everyone can easily read the content.

2. As a group, establish connections between ideas:
   • Draw lines or arrows between similar or process-related items.
   • Circle important concepts.
   • Number items as needed.

   Another option is to create a mind map to organize this information.

3. Once you have organized your ideas, synthesize the content to produce a statement of your definite major purpose. Make sure to frame your definite chief aim as an opportunity to be realized, not a challenge to be overcome.

ACTION ITEMS

- Save the mind map or conceptual diagram that results from today's brain-storming session to bring to the next meeting.
- Transfer the statement of your Master Mind's definite major purpose to an index or business card. Make enough copies so that every member can carry a card with them.
- At least twice a day, every member should take out this card and read the Master Mind's chief aim out loud, in full confidence that their collective purpose will be accomplished.

Notes

ACQUIRING SPECIALIZED KNOWLEDGE

TODAY'S OUTCOME

Determine what specialized knowledge
you will require—and where you can obtain it.

FLOW ACTIVITY

Ask members to reflect on, and then share their answers to, the following question: What is one piece of knowledge or skill that you didn't think would be useful when you acquired it, but that ultimately served you greatly?

MEETING AGENDA

1. Before the meeting commences, display the mind map or conceptual diagram from the last session so that everyone can easily read the content.

2. Ask group members to survey the conceptual diagram and share their thoughts on the following:
   • What elements should be researched to better ascertain how they will contribute to the Master Mind's larger goal?
   • Where can we obtain this specialized knowledge?

3. Create a list of the specialized knowledge that will be required to achieve your group's definite major purpose.

4. Next, determine who should be tasked with locating each element of specialized knowledge that is needed. Assign research tasks to individual members and provide a timeline for obtaining the information. Note that half of the members will be expected to share their findings in session 6 and the other half in session 7.

ACTION ITEMS

■ Create a plan for obtaining the knowledge you have been tasked with acquiring. Ask yourself:
  • What knowledge do I already have?
  • What knowledge do I need?
  • What print or online sources can I consult to obtain this knowledge?
  • Which individuals can I consult to obtain this knowledge?
  • What steps do I need to take to acquire all the necessary knowledge?
■ Do your research! Take steps to accomplish your plan and acquire knowledge to share with your Master Mind group.
■ Visualize your attainment of the Master Mind's definite major purpose, claiming the group's success by speaking your purpose with full faith in its achievement.

Notes

EVALUATING INFORMATION

TODAY'S OUTCOME

Create guidelines for evaluating specialized knowledge
from Master Mind members.

FLOW ACTIVITY

Ask everyone to describe a time when they had an assumption or a bias challenged by their exposure to new ideas, information, or individuals.

Alternately, you can ask members to define *tolerance* in their own words and describe how they live out this value in their daily lives.

MEETING AGENDA

1. Determine as a group how you will verify that the specialized knowledge members obtain is both (1) accurate and (2) relevant to the group's chief aim.

2. Create a list of guidelines for assessing information for its credibility and relevance.

ACTION ITEMS

- Ask half of the members to share their assigned specialized knowledge at the next session.
- Make one new connection, or reach out to one individual, who can provide insight on the specialized knowledge you require.
- Continue to visualize your attainment of the Master Mind's definite major purpose, claiming the group's success by speaking your purpose with full faith in its achievement.

Notes

EXCHANGING RESEARCH FINDINGS—DAY 1

TODAY'S OUTCOME

Share and evaluate members' findings and incorporate them
into your picture of the Master Mind's larger goal.

FLOW ACTIVITY

Ask everyone to share about a book that greatly shaped their perspective or
perhaps even transformed their life. Invite everyone to give a brief (1–3 sentence)
synopsis of the book and an explanation of its impact on their life.

MEETING AGENDA

1. Ask the members who brought specialized knowledge to take turns sharing
   what they learned.

2. After everyone has presented their findings, apply the guidelines for evaluating
   specialized knowledge to ensure the information presented is (1) credible
   and (2) relevant. Discard any information that does not meet both of these
   requirements.

3. Work as a group to integrate the approved specialized knowledge into the
   Master Mind's conceptualization of its definite major purpose. From this step
   you should emerge with a more developed picture of the various components
   necessary to achieve the group's larger goal.

ACTION ITEMS

- Ask the other half of the members to share their assigned specialized knowledge
  at the next session.

- Have members read one new chapter, article, or book of their own choosing on the subject of the Master Mind's definite major purpose.
- Continue to visualize your attainment of the Master Mind's definite major purpose, claiming the group's success by speaking your purpose with full faith in its achievement.

Notes

EXCHANGING RESEARCH FINDINGS—DAY 2

TODAY'S OUTCOME

Share and evaluate members' findings and incorporate them
into your picture of the Master Mind's larger goal.

FLOW ACTIVITY

Ask members to interview the person sitting next to them to learn their answer to the following question: What businessperson, innovator, thought leader, or cultural icon do you most admire, and why? Share with the rest of the group what you discover about the other person.

MEETING AGENDA

1. Ask the members who brought specialized knowledge to take turns sharing what they learned.

2. After everyone has presented their findings, apply the guidelines for evaluating specialized knowledge to ensure the information presented is (1) credible and (2) relevant. Discard any information that does not meet both of these requirements.

3. Work as a group to integrate the approved specialized knowledge into the Master Mind's conceptualization of its definite major purpose. From this step you should emerge with a more developed picture of the various components necessary to achieve the group's larger goal.

ACTION ITEMS

- Create a document that explains how all the approved specialized knowledge provided by members informs the Master Mind's understanding of its definite major purpose.
- Continue to visualize your attainment of the Master Mind's definite major purpose, claiming the group's success by speaking your purpose with full faith in its achievement.

Notes

IDENTIFYING NECESSARY ACTION STEPS

TODAY'S OUTCOME

Determine what action steps will be needed to accomplish
the alliance's definite major purpose.

FLOW ACTIVITY

As a group, discuss your answer to the following questions: How do you define
legacy? What sort of legacy do you intend to leave? Who will benefit from this
legacy?

MEETING AGENDA

1. Work together to identify the action steps you will need to take to accomplish
   the Master Mind's definite major purpose. At this point, you are not trying to
   organize the steps into a specific order, nor are you trying to create a plan or
   timeline. You are merely trying to determine the actions you will need to take
   to achieve your primary aim. To do this, answer the following questions as a
   group:
   • What are our larger goals, and how can we break these down into smaller
     ones?
   • What specific actions will be required to realize these smaller goals?
   • How long can we reasonably expect each step to take?

2. Create a list or conceptual diagram that maps out the group's larger goals,
   smaller goals, actions required to accomplish each goal, and the anticipated
   time every action will take.

ACTION ITEMS

- Give each Master Mind member a copy of the list or diagram created in step 2 and ask them to think about the most effective order for the action steps.
- Assign everyone a chapter or article to read that will inspire personal growth or increase specialized knowledge relevant to the focus of the Master Mind. This reading will be discussed at the next Master Mind meeting.
- Continue to visualize your attainment of the Master Mind's definite major purpose, claiming the group's success by speaking your purpose with full faith in its achievement.

Notes

_____

_____

_____

_____

_____

_____

_____

_____

_____

_____

_____

_____

_____

_____

_____

_____

_____

_____

_____

_____

_____

_____

_____

_____

_____

_____

_____

_____

IDENTIFYING NECESSARY RESOURCES

TODAY'S OUTCOME

Determine what resources will be needed to accomplish
the alliance's definite major purpose.

FLOW ACTIVITY

Discuss the assigned reading that everyone explored as one of their action items from the last session. In your conversation, make sure to address:
- Your key takeaway from the reading
- One passage that really stood out to you (read the quotation aloud)
- How the reading illuminated your understanding of, or approach to, the Master Mind's major purpose
- How you can translate the knowledge gained from it into action

MEETING AGENDA

1. Work together to identify the resources you will need to take to accomplish the Master Mind's definite major purpose. To do this, display the conceptual diagram or list created in the last Master Mind session so that everyone can see it, and answer the following questions as a group:
   - What resources (financial, material, people, technological, etc.) are needed to achieve our smaller goals?
   - How can we obtain these resources? Who will be responsible for attaining and managing each necessary resource?
   - When can these resources be obtained?

2. Next to every smaller goal on the conceptual diagram or list, add the resources that will be required to accomplish it, the person responsible for securing it, and the deadline for its procurement.

ACTION ITEMS

- Continue thinking about the most effective order for the action steps required to accomplish the Master Mind's definite major purpose.
- Work on procuring the resource(s) for which you are responsible by its due date.
- Continue to visualize your attainment of the Master Mind's definite major purpose, claiming the group's success by speaking your purpose with full faith in its achievement.

Notes

BRAINSTORMING A PROVISIONAL PLAN—DAY 1

TODAY'S OUTCOME

Create part 1 of a provisional plan to achieve your group's definite major purpose.

FLOW ACTIVITY

As a group, discuss your answer to the following questions: What is one new hobby you would like to acquire? What about this hobby is appealing to you? Does it connect at all with your definite major purpose (even if it's just to fuel your creativity or adaptability)?

After members share their responses, briefly exchange ideas for initial steps each person can take to begin enjoying their desired hobby.

MEETING AGENDA

1. Using the conceptual diagram or list of necessary action steps and required resources you created and expanded on in previous sessions, collectively brainstorm the first portion of a provisional plan to attain your group's definite chief aim. Today, you'll outline the following components of your plan:
   - Definite steps whose success can be verified before moving on
   - Deadlines by which each step must be completed

   You should emerge from this session with a clear, step-by-step plan for accomplishing your Master Mind's primary goal.

ACTION ITEMS

■ Convert the list of steps you created in today's Master Mind session into a mind map or timeline that visually depicts the various steps involved in accomplishing your major purpose. Distribute a copy of this diagram to every member, and bring it to all future Master Mind sessions.

■ Continue to visualize your attainment of the Master Mind's definite major purpose, claiming the group's success by speaking your purpose with full faith in its achievement.

Notes

BRAINSTORMING A
PROVISIONAL PLAN—DAY 2

TODAY'S OUTCOME

Create part 2 of a provisional plan to achieve your group's definite major purpose.

FLOW ACTIVITY

As a group, discuss your answer to the following questions: If you could travel anywhere in the world, where would it be—and why?

Consider whether anyone in the group has connections that could make this dream trip happen.

MEETING AGENDA

1. Using the conceptual diagram or list of necessary action steps and required resources you created and expanded on in previous sessions, collectively brainstorm the second portion of a provisional plan to attain your group's definite chief aim. Today, you'll add the following component to your plan:

   • A definition of success for each step

2. Create guidelines for what the group will do when a step has not been completed satisfactorily.

ACTION ITEMS

■ Assign everyone a chapter or article to read that will inspire personal growth or increase specialized knowledge relevant to the focus of the Master Mind. This reading will be discussed at the next Master Mind meeting.

■ Continue to visualize your attainment of the Master Mind's definite major purpose, claiming the group's success by speaking your purpose with full faith in its achievement.

Notes

BRAINSTORMING A
PROVISIONAL PLAN—DAY 3

Create part 3 of a provisional plan to achieve your group's definite major purpose.

FLOW ACTIVITY

Discuss the assigned reading that everyone explored as one of their action items from the last session. In your conversation, make sure to address:
- Your key takeaway from the reading
- One passage that really stood out to you (read the quotation aloud)
- How the reading illuminated your understanding of, or approach to, the Master Mind's major purpose
- How you can translate the knowledge gained from it into action

MEETING AGENDA

1. Using the conceptual diagram or list of necessary action steps and required resources you created and expanded on in previous sessions, collectively brainstorm the final portion of a provisional plan to attain your group's definite chief aim. Today, you'll complete the working draft of your plan by adding these last few elements:
   - Statements of what each person and/or the group as a whole is willing to give in return for the completion of each step (time, resources, effort, etc.). In other words, what's the trade-off? As Hill reminds us in *Think and Grow Rich*, "There is no such reality as 'something for nothing.'"[34]
   - A manager responsible for coordinating the progress of each step and ensuring its timely completion

ACTION ITEMS

- Reflect on the step(s) you've been assigned to manage and outline a plan for ensuring its success.
- Continue to visualize your attainment of the Master Mind's definite major purpose, claiming the group's success by speaking your purpose with full faith in its achievement.

Notes

PERFORMING A SWOT ANALYSIS ON THE PROVISIONAL PLAN

TODAY'S OUTCOME

Evaluate the strength of your proposed plan for achieving your alliance's chief aim by performing a SWOT analysis.

FLOW ACTIVITY

Ask all members to share their answer to the following question: What is one thing the group doesn't know about you that you would like us to know?

MEETING AGENDA

1. Divide members into four groups. Task each group with answering ONE of the following questions in a specified amount of time (e.g., 20 minutes):

   - **What are the strengths of our proposed plan?** How is it based on solid research and analysis? How is it the best use of our resources? How does it offer a reasonable timeline for completion that also challenges us? How is it unique? What benefits will it produce that will support the attainment of our major goal? How will it serve others?

   - **What are the weaknesses of our provisional plan?** Have we made any assumptions that could undercut our progress? How are resources being wasted or at least not maximized? Do we lack necessary resources and could we struggle to obtain them? Do any timelines need to be adjusted? Are there any internal or external factors for which we did not account? Are any of the steps too vague?

   - **What opportunities will be created by this plan?** What new options will result as we complete each step? What opportunities can we take advantage of to ensure our ultimate success?

- **What threats might thwart our progress?** What threats, both internal and external to the group, might cause us to lose momentum? Are we competing with anyone, and if so, might they cause any interference? What risks are involved?

2. Reconvene the larger group session and discuss your answers. Press into the insights: challenge them, expand upon them, make them more specific—ultimately, refine them. Save this document and bring it to your next Master Mind meeting.

ACTION ITEMS

- Scrutinize the working draft of your plan in individual brainstorming sessions. Concentrate on your major purpose and analyze whether any element of the plan needs to be revised or improved upon.
- Continue to visualize your attainment of the Master Mind's definite major purpose, claiming the group's success by speaking your purpose with full faith in its achievement.

Notes

REFINING YOUR PLAN

TODAY'S OUTCOME

Refine your plan for attaining the Master Mind's definite major purpose
in light of the information gleaned from your SWOT analysis.

FLOW ACTIVITY

Ask all members to share their answer to the following questions: What is one
food or activity you haven't tried yet? Why haven't you tried it—what's holding
you back?

Help each other commit to going out of your comfort zone and trying something
new—unless, of course, there are allergies, intolerances, or other medical or
safety reasons for avoiding that food or activity.

MEETING AGENDA

1. Take each step of your provisional plan and determine whether it needs to
   be revised based on the results of your SWOT analysis. Before making any
   changes, consider:
   - Does this change *need* to be made to improve our outcome? (Remember,
     it's important to be quick to make decisions but slow to change them.)
   - Will this change improve the speed with which we will accomplish our goal
     without sacrificing the quality of the result?
   - Will this change require more or less resources? How will that affect our
     results?
   - Will this change require someone else to be in charge of the relevant goal?

2. Create a new written document outlining the details of your group's plan.

ACTION ITEMS

- Photocopy the newly revised plan and distribute it to all members. Make sure to bring a copy of this plan to all future Master Mind sessions.
- Determine whether the steps you've been assigned to manage have changed in any way and decide what new steps you need to take to ensure their success— and act on them immediately!
- Continue to visualize your attainment of the Master Mind's definite major purpose, claiming the group's success by speaking your purpose with full faith in its achievement.

Notes

_____

_____

_____

_____

_____

_____

_____

_____

_____

_____

_____

_____

_____

_____

_____

_____

_____

_____

_____

_____

_____

_____

_____

_____

_____

CHECKING IN WITH THE GOAL MANAGERS

Facilitate a feedback session on each goal manager's strategy.

FLOW ACTIVITY

For this activity, you will need a whiteboard, chalkboard, flip chart, or large piece of paper. Give all members a writing utensil and ask them to write all the words they can think of that they associate with the word *accountability*. After everyone is done, the Master Mind leader should facilitate a brief conversation about the words people chose:

• Which words surprised you?
• Which words were repeated?
• Which words relate to each other in interesting ways?

Based on this discussion, attempt to create a short definition of *accountability*. Ask members to keep this definition in mind when reflecting on the goal(s) for which they are responsible.

MEETING AGENDA

1. Check in with members on the goal(s) for which they're responsible. Ask them to share their answers to the following questions:
   • What progress have you made on it/them?
   • Are you on schedule to complete each step on time?
   • What actions still need to be taken?
   • To whom could you delegate some of the work?
   • Have you encountered any challenges (read: opportunities)?
   • Do you require additional support to accomplish this goal? If so, what kind?

2. Allow time for members to share their insight about what would enhance each individual's ability to ensure the success of the goal(s) for which they are responsible.

ACTION ITEMS

- Revise your approach to managing your goal(s) based on the counsel of the other Master Mind Members—and continue taking action!
- Prepare to share one action you've taken toward the attainment of the group's major purpose at the next Master Mind session.
- Continue to visualize your attainment of the Master Mind's definite major purpose, claiming the group's success by speaking your purpose with full faith in its achievement.

Notes

TAKING DEFINITE ACTION

Support each other in taking more definite steps
to achieve the Master Mind's major purpose.

FLOW ACTIVITY

Today's flow activity is a mindfulness exercise. Have someone set a timer for three minutes. Ask members to spend that time focusing on their breathing and intentionally placing the group's definite major purpose front of mind. Ask them to notice any thoughts—both relevant and irrelevant to your purpose—that arise. Accept them as they come, and then let them go. After the time is up, members should share their reflections on and experience with this exercise.

MEETING AGENDA

1. Ask members to discuss one specific action they have taken since the last meeting to make progress on the Master Mind's major purpose. In their discussion, they should mention:
   • The specific steps involved in that action
   • The reason behind the approach they took
   • The mindset they adopted for completing the action
   • The outcome of their action

2. Allow time for members to share their insight on the steps each member has taken to support the group's larger goal.

ACTION ITEMS

- Revise your approach to managing your goal(s) based on the counsel of other Master Mind Members—and continue taking action!
- Have everyone read a chapter or article that will inspire personal growth or increase specialized knowledge on the focus of the Master Mind. This will be discussed at the next Master Mind meeting.
- Continue to visualize your attainment of the Master Mind's definite major purpose, claiming the group's success by speaking your purpose with full faith in its achievement.

Notes

_____

_____

_____

_____

_____

_____

_____

_____

_____

_____

_____

_____

_____

_____

_____

_____

_____

_____

_____

_____

_____

_____

_____

MAINTAINING MOTIVATION

TODAY'S OUTCOME

Increase "stickability" so that members remain committed
to achieving the group's larger goal.

FLOW ACTIVITY

Ask members to share one time they gave up on something too early: What was their reasoning for throwing in the towel when they did? What was the result? What could have been the result had they persevered a little longer?

MEETING AGENDA

1. Invite members to share any instances of temporary defeat they have encountered in attempting to achieve the Master Mind's definite major purpose.

2. Engage the creative imagination to collectively determine how these instances of temporary defeat contain seeds of greater opportunities. To do so, consider:
   • Is there a lesson to be learned from this challenge?
   • Is there a sign that we could revise our strategy for greater success?
   • Is there a connection or resource that could be gained through this experience?
   • What has this experience taught me about myself and my inner strength that could be leveraged to accomplish something greater in the future?

ACTION ITEMS

▪ Read the story of R. U. Darby, found in Napoleon Hill's *Think and Grow Rich*, and ponder the value of persisting when you're only "Three Feet from Gold."

- Write a list of reasons you are committed to attaining the Master Mind's definite major purpose—be specific! What will help you stay committed when your motivation is waning?
- Continue to visualize your attainment of the Master Mind's definite major purpose, claiming the group's success by speaking your purpose with full faith in its achievement.

Notes

EXPANDING INNOVATION

Discover creative ways to achieve your Master Mind's larger goal.

FLOW ACTIVITY

Ask members to discuss the following questions: In your opinion, what person or organization provides the best service? How do they do this? What is unique about the value they add?

MEETING AGENDA

The goal of today's session is to determine whether the Master Mind's goals could be achieved in a more creative way.

1. To do this, the leader should start by introducing the concepts of the synthetic imagination and the creative imagination. According to Hill:
   • The synthetic imagination rearranges existing knowledge to produce new combinations.
   • The creative imagination delivers "hunches" or "flashes" of inspiration that contain entirely new ideas.
   For further reading, see "Two Forms of Imagination" in *Think and Grow Rich*.

2. Then, the leader should facilitate a group brainstorming session that explores the following questions:
   • How could we take some of what's really great about the person or organization we discussed in our flow activity and apply that insight to our efforts in this Master Mind?

- How could we add value in more unique ways by combining different ideas to produce something new (synthetic imagination)?
- How could we add value in more unique ways by generating a completely new idea (creative imagination)?

ACTION ITEMS

■ Assign everyone a chapter or article to read that will inspire personal growth or increase specialized knowledge relevant to the focus of the Master Mind. This reading will be discussed at the next Master Mind meeting.

■ Continue to visualize your attainment of the Master Mind's definite major purpose, claiming the group's success by speaking your purpose with full faith in its achievement.

Notes

MOBILIZING DESIRE

TODAY'S OUTCOME

Continue activating the creative imagination through
the controlled use of strong, positive emotions.

FLOW ACTIVITY

Discuss the assigned reading that everyone explored as one of their action items
from the last session. In your conversation, make sure to address:

- Your key takeaway from the reading
- One passage that really stood out to you (read the quotation aloud)
- How the reading illuminated your understanding of, or approach to, the
  Master Mind's major purpose
- How you can translate the knowledge gained from it into action

MEETING AGENDA

1. Read and reflect on the following passage from *Napoleon Hill's The Language
   of Thought*:

   *When the conscious mind is vibrating at an exceedingly rapid rate, as through
   the presence of strong emotion, the creative imagination begins receiving thought
   impulses from the ether, both from Infinite Intelligence and from others' minds,
   and processes them to generate new plans for attaining your definite chief aim.
   Emotions, then, are responsible for opening a direct line of communication
   between finite man and the Infinite (universal intelligence), and they are a
   required ingredient for creativity, which is necessary to conceiving practical plans
   of action.*[35]

2. Make a list of positive emotions that members believe to be constructive. Alternatively, you might choose to focus on "The Seven Major Positive Emotions" provided by Hill:
   - The emotion of DESIRE
   - The emotion of FAITH
   - The emotion of LOVE
   - The emotion of SEX
   - The emotion of ENTHUSIASM
   - The emotion of ROMANCE
   - The emotion of HOPE

3. For each emotion, determine how it can be used to inspire the pursuit of the Master Mind's definite purpose. For example, with the emotion of desire, consider what images and experiences create intense longing in your heart and mind and how they could connect with the group's chief aim.

4. Spend time as a group applying these emotions to the Master Mind's definite major purpose. Raise the level of vibration of your collective thoughts by holding the feelings in your mind alongside the thought of accomplishing your major purpose.

5. Share and discuss any revelations that result from this exercise.

ACTION ITEMS

- Take an inventory of your personal habits and identify three constructive ones and three destructive ones. Bring this list to the next Master Mind session.
- Continue to visualize your attainment of the Master Mind's definite major purpose, claiming the group's success by speaking your purpose with full faith in its achievement.

Notes

BUILDING BETTER PERSONAL HABITS

Identify habits that are not serving you personally
and replace them with more constructive ones.

FLOW ACTIVITY

As a group, explore what goes into forming and breaking habits. Discuss the following:

- Do you tend to form habits consciously or unknowingly?
- When you realize a habit is not serving you, what do you do?
- How do you weed out destructive habits and replace them with constructive habits?

MEETING AGENDA

1. Take turns sharing about your constructive and destructive habits. You might organize the discussion around different types of habits. For example:
   - Health-related habits
   - Financial habits
   - Habits of thought
   - Habits of speech
   - Relational habits

2. Help each other create an action plan for replacing destructive habits with constructive ones.

ACTION ITEMS

- Take an inventory of your professional habits and identify three constructive ones and three destructive ones. Bring this list to the next Master Mind session.
- Implement the thoughts and behaviors you discussed in today's session to convert your destructive personal habits into constructive ones.
- Continue to visualize your attainment of the Master Mind's definite major purpose, claiming the group's success by speaking your purpose with full faith in its achievement.

Notes

_____

_____

_____

_____

_____

_____

_____

_____

_____

_____

_____

_____

_____

_____

_____

_____

_____

_____

_____

_____

_____

_____

_____

_____

_____

_____

_____

_____

BUILDING BETTER PROFESSIONAL HABITS

TODAY'S OUTCOME

Identify habits that are not serving you professionally
and replace them with more constructive ones.

FLOW ACTIVITY

As a group, reflect on and discuss the following passages from Hill's *Outwitting the Devil*:

> *Habits come in pairs, triplets and quadruplets. Any habit which weakens one's will-power invites quadruplets. Any habit which weakens one's will-power invites a flock of its relatives to move in and take possession of the mind.*[36]

> *The mind is nothing more than the sum total of one's habits!*[37]

What is the connection between thought and action? How can you control your thoughts to take control of your actions and outcomes?

MEETING AGENDA

1. Take turns sharing about your constructive and destructive work-related habits. You might organize the discussion around different types of professional habits. For example:
   - Habits of productivity or procrastination
   - Leadership habits
   - Professional communication habits

2. Help each other create an action plan for replacing destructive habits with constructive ones.

ACTION ITEMS

- Assign everyone a chapter or article to read that will inspire personal growth or increase specialized knowledge relevant to the focus of the Master Mind. This reading will be discussed at the next Master Mind meeting.
- Implement the thoughts and behaviors you discussed in today's session to convert your destructive professional habits into constructive ones.
- Continue to visualize your attainment of the Master Mind's definite major purpose, claiming the group's success by speaking your purpose with full faith in its achievement.

Notes

ENSURING CONTINUED ACTION

TODAY'S OUTCOME

Support each other in taking more definite steps
to achieve the Master Mind's major purpose.

FLOW ACTIVITY

Discuss the assigned reading that everyone explored as one of their action items from the last session. In your conversation, make sure to address:

- Your key takeaway from the reading
- One passage that really stood out to you (read the quotation aloud)
- How the reading illuminated your understanding of, or approach to, the Master Mind's major purpose
- How you can translate the knowledge gained from it into action

MEETING AGENDA

1. Ask members to discuss one specific action they have taken recently to make progress on the Master Mind's major purpose. In their discussion, they should mention:
   - The specific steps involved in that action
   - The reason behind the approach they took
   - The mindset they adopted for completing the action
   - The outcome of their action

2. Allow time for members to share their insight on the steps each member has taken to support the group's larger goal.

ACTION ITEMS

- Revise your approach to managing your goal(s) based on the counsel of the other Master Mind Members—and continue taking action!
- Think about one area of your business or personal life in which you are selling yourself short. Be prepared to share this in the next Master Mind session.
- Continue to visualize your attainment of the Master Mind's definite major purpose, claiming the group's success by speaking your purpose with full faith in its achievement.

Notes

SUPPORTING PERSONAL GROWTH

TODAY'S OUTCOME

Identify at least one way that you are selling yourself short—
and start claiming more space in that area.

FLOW ACTIVITY

For this activity, you will need a flip chart, whiteboard, or other large canvas and a writing utensil. Ask members to share the *one* word they feel best describes how their success journey is going. As they share, write their words on the canvas you're using. After everyone has had their turn, facilitate a conversation about the words that were given:

- Are those the words the individuals would like to use to describe their success journey? If not, what is their most desired adjective?
- Does anyone need encouragement?
- Is there a pattern that could be addressed?

MEETING AGENDA

1. Ask members to share about the area in which they feel they are selling themselves short, whether by not taking risks, not investing enough resources (time, energy, money) in themselves and their dreams, not being more assertive, etc.

2. Help individuals create a game plan for claiming what they desire. Consider:
   - Is there a self-confidence issue that needs to be corrected?
   - Is there a logistical problem that could be resolved?
   - What opportunities are evident that could be realized?
   - What opportunities could be created?

ACTION ITEMS

- Implement the game plan recommended by your fellow Master Mind members and record the results of your endeavors. Remember: your thoughts create your reality—don't sell yourself short!
- Continue to visualize your attainment of the Master Mind's definite major purpose, claiming the group's success by speaking your purpose with full faith in its achievement.

Notes

CULTIVATING GRATITUDE

TODAY'S OUTCOME

Develop more gratitude for the areas in which you are already wealthy.

FLOW ACTIVITY

For this activity, you will need a flip chart, whiteboard, or other large canvas and a writing utensil. Ask members to share the *one* word they feel best describes what it means to be wealthy. As they share, write their words on the canvas you're using. After everyone has had their turn, facilitate a conversation about the words that were given:

- Are there similarities? Differences? What do the consistencies and inconsistencies reveal?
- Do people primarily view success as a material reality or an emotional/spiritual one? What does that reveal?
- What definition of wealth would be most conducive to sustainable success and happiness? Why?

MEETING AGENDA

1. Ask members to share three ways they are wealthy *at this very moment*. Consider all forms of wealth:
   - Material • Financial • Emotional • Spiritual • Relational

2. Allow each member time to write a statement of gratitude for these three forms of wealth. Share these statements with each other.

ACTION ITEMS

- Speak your gratitude statement out loud at least once every day.
- Continue to visualize your attainment of the Master Mind's definite major purpose, claiming the group's success by speaking your purpose with full faith in its achievement.

Notes

GOING THE EXTRA MILE

TODAY'S OUTCOME

Determine ways you can maximize your success by going the extra mile.

FLOW ACTIVITY

Read the following excerpt from Napoleon Hill's radio lecture on "Going the Extra Mile":

> *"Going the extra mile," as it constitutes a part of this philosophy, means that you render more service and better service than you're paid to render, but you do it all the time and in a fine, friendly spirit.*[38]

Then, discuss: How would you define "going the extra mile"? What does it mean to you? Do you think the attitude in which you render this service is as important as the action of serving? Why or why not?

MEETING AGENDA

1. Ask members to brainstorm and share ideas about how they can go the extra mile in their...
   - personal life (*relationships, community service, organizations to which they belong*)
   - professional life (*as an employee, as a leader, as an innovator*)

   Where are there other opportunities to serve others by committing time, money, and/or effort? How can members realize these opportunities?

2. Help each other make a plan to start going the extra mile in at least one of these areas this week.

ACTION ITEMS

- Take action on your blueprint for going the extra mile. Journal about the following: How did it serve others? How did it serve you? What new opportunities arose from it?
- Make a list of what you are hoping to get out of the Master Mind as it moves forward. Brainstorm ideas to strengthen its power.
- Continue to visualize your attainment of the Master Mind's definite major purpose, claiming the group's success by speaking your purpose with full faith in its achievement.

Notes

REFLECTING AND PROGRESSING

TODAY'S OUTCOME

Reflect on what you have achieved in your alliance
and make plans to attain further progress.

FLOW ACTIVITY

Ask members to share something that has changed about them—or for them—
as a result of their participation in the Master Mind group up to this point.

MEETING AGENDA

1. Evaluate your progress on the Master Mind's definite major goal:
   - Did you achieve it yet? If not, are you on track to achieve it by your established deadline?
   - What obstacles did you encounter? How did you overcome them?
   - What can you celebrate about your journey thus far?
   - Did everyone benefit from the group's success?
   - What, if anything, would you do differently next time?

2. Outline future plans that should be established. Consider:
   - Is there a new major goal to set?
   - Are there smaller goals that should be added to help us attain our definite chief aim?
   - What actions should we take now to accomplish our primary goal?
   - Should the structure of this Master Mind change or stay the same?

ACTION ITEMS

- Make a list of ways you can better support your fellow Master Mind members as the group enters its next phase.
- If it hasn't yet been achieved, continue to visualize your attainment of the Master Mind's definite major purpose, claiming the group's success by speaking your purpose with full faith in its achievement.

Notes

CONCLUSION
Sustainable Master Mind Living

Now that you understand the incredible power of the Master Mind, be intentional about continuing to organize and direct it effectively so that the power is used constructively. Keep in mind:

- Harmony is the most crucial ingredient in a Master Mind alliance. Without it, a Master Mind will never succeed in its aims.

- A Master Mind must remain active to accomplish its purpose. This requires regular meetings—with all members present—and consistent action outside of the meetings toward the attainment of the alliance's definite aim.

Harmony and action—these are the watchwords of an effective Master Mind alliance. Live out the principles described in this book day after day, aligning your thoughts and deeds with the group's major purpose, and tune in to the inspiration that will come to you for bolder moves and stronger plans. Remember…

> **"No individual may have great power without availing himself [or herself] of the 'Master Mind.'"**[39]

If an individual depended on his or her efforts alone to accomplish a large goal, that person would find it nearly impossible to assemble the necessary knowledge and express it through definite plans of action.

But that's not all…

Think not only of the amazing benefits in store for you when you participate in a Master Mind. Think, too, of the value it will add to your colleagues, your community, and even the larger world. As Hill shares in *The Science of Personal Achievement*:

One of the greatest benefits of this philosophy for you and those with whom you connect and the world around you is to teach people how to live with one another under the Master Mind principle, so you and they have more joy in living. They, like you, will have more prosperity, better health, and will make this a better country in which to live."[40]

More joy, more prosperity, better health, and a better community—these riches and countless others await you as you continually exercise the Master Mind principle.

NOTES

1. Napoleon Hill, *The Science of Personal Achievement* (Shippensburg, PA: Sound Wisdom, 2022), xiii.
2. Ibid., 15.
3. Napoleon Hill, *Think Your Way to Wealth* (Shippensburg, PA: Sound Wisdom, 2022), 17.
4. Ibid., 20.
5. Ibid., 21.
6. Napoleon Hill, *The Law of Success* (Shippensburg, PA: Sound Wisdom, 2021), 28.
7. Hill, *Think Your Way to Wealth*, 22.
8. Hill, *Science of Personal Achievement*, 25.
9. Hill, *Law of Success*, 32.
10. Napoleon Hill, *Think and Grow Rich* (Shippensburg, PA: Sound Wisdom, 2017), 108.
11. Ibid., 107.
12. Hill, *Law of Success*, 28.
13. Hill, *Science of Personal Achievement*, 68.
14. Ibid., 65.
15. Ibid., 66.
16. Ibid.
17. Ibid., 68–69.
18. Ibid., 70.
19. Hill, *Science of Personal Achievement*, 26.
20. Ibid., 41.
21. Hill, *Think and Grow Rich*, 230.
22. Hill, *Science of Personal Achievement*, 41.
23. Ibid., 18.
24. Hill, *The Law of Success*, 33.
25. Ibid., 28.
26. Hill, *Science of Personal Achievement*, 15.
27. Ibid., 27.
28. Ibid., 25.
29. Ibid., 26.
30. Hill, *The Law of Success*, 40.
31. Hill, *Think Your Way to Wealth*, 24.
32. Napoleon Hill, *Outwitting the Devil* (Shippensburg, PA: Sound Wisdom, 2020), 195.
33. Hill, *Think and Grow Rich*, 211.
34. Ibid., 42.
35. Napoleon Hill, *The Language of Thought* (Shippensburg, PA: Sound Wisdom, 2022), 34.
36. Hill, *Outwitting the Devil*, 105.
37. Ibid., 113.
38. Napoleon Hill, "Going the Extra Mile," in *Napoleon Hill's Greatest Speeches*, 215–44 (Shippensburg, PA: Sound Wisdom, 2016).
39. Hill, *Think and Grow Rich*, 251.
40. Hill, *Science of Personal Achievement*, 38.

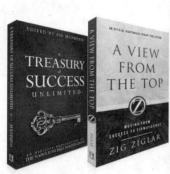
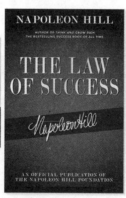